Performance Management

10 Steps to Getting the Most from Your Workforce

Clive Lewis OBE DL

First published in 2012

By

Globis Ltd
Unit 1
Wheatstone Court
Waterwells Business Park
Quedgeley
Gloucester
GL2 2AQ

ISBN 978-0-9568648-8-8

Cover design by Brendan Vaughan-Spruce

Printed and bound in the UK by

Berforts Information Press
23-25 Gunnels Wood Park
Stevenage
Hertfordshire
SG1 2BH

Index

Index

Introduction

The importance of performance management to an organisation cannot be underestimated. An individual, team or organisation that doesn't have regular targets to aim for, methods in place allowing them to get there and help available when problems arise will soon find themselves hit hard where it matters – the bottom line. Organisations who offer inadequate performance management (or none at all) may find that underperformance is not spotted and dealt with, which can lead to a lack of care and pride in an employee's work, with an obvious impact on the team and therefore ultimately the organisation. The longer this attitude is left to fester the more difficult it will be to reverse when the problems come to light. Not only can this lead to talented individuals deserting the company but the wrong sort of people can be recruited to take their place. Performance management therefore acts as a preventative tool for long-term performance issues as well as a ladder to further success. It is important to articulate to managers, especially line managers, what the objective of the performance management approach is. Often managers seem confused about this and it can lead to inconsistency in treatment and conflict.

Performance management is a term that has been in use since the 1950s, but many still struggle to define

Individuals, teams or organisations that don't have regularly reviewed targets and methods of achieving them will seldom progress effectively.

If underperformance is not spotted soon it can filter through the organisation and can be difficult to reverse. A performance management strategy can help prevent this.

Performance management has been in use since the 1950s, but it looks very different now to how it did when first coined.

what it actually is. This may be for two principle reasons; firstly because it is not one specific thing, rather an umbrella term for a range of processes and systems designed to evaluate and improve organisation performance, and secondly because performance management has changed so much since its initial introduction into the workplace in over 60 years that it no longer means what it used to.

Performance management covers a range of processes rather than just being an individual process itself.

Performance management was initially used as a method of equating and justifying employee salaries, but this approach was deemed too focused on financial reward and ignored those motivated by other rewards. Performance management, when done well, now covers a range of personal objectives, targets and motivations to meet the diverse needs of the billions of employees that make up the modern workforce.

Performance management was initially used as a method of equating and justifying employee salaries.

The lack of understanding given to performance management is evident by the lack of an official definition of the subject. The following definition however is offered by the University of Indiana and is one of the better ones:

No official definition is given for performance management.

"Performance management is an ongoing, continuous process of communicating and clarifying job responsibilities, priorities and performance expectations in order to ensure mutual understanding between supervisor and employee. It is a philosophy which values and encourages employee development

through a style of management which provides frequent feedback and fosters teamwork. It emphasizes communication and focuses on adding value to the organization by promoting improved job performance and encouraging skill development. Performance Management involves clarifying the job duties, defining performance standards, and documenting, evaluating and discussing performance with each employee."[1]

This description recognises the many derivatives of performance management that exist today, which is not an easy task considering the myriad of ways in which performance management is adapted, tweaked and individualised depending on the requirements of the organisation in question. Performance management, then, is not a 'thing' but a combination of systems and processes brought together in order to improve performance, achieve goals and measure progress. This sounds simple in theory, but in practice effective performance management implementation requires a variety of skills and complete co-operation from all levels of the organisation. It relies on each individual striving to reach their specific goals, from which team, department and consequently organisational success should follow. Thus each individual has a direct responsibility for organisational achievement no matter how large or small the part they play, encouraging them to feel a sense of personal

"Performance management is an ongoing, continuous process of communicating and clarifying job responsibilities, priorities and performance expectations in order to ensure mutual understanding between supervisor and employee."

Performance management is not a 'thing' but a combination of systems and processes brought together in order to improve performance, achieve goals and measure progress.

Effective performance management relies on each individual striving to reach specific goals from which team, department and consequently organisational success should follow.

pride at the company's overall success. This fosters a positive attitude and a sense of personal responsibility, from which everyone benefits.

The best performance management strategies utilise a number of elements to cover a range of skills and targets and are tailored to departments, teams and individuals of all levels. Frameworks are drawn up in the planning stages that utilise where possible existing HR policies and performance indicators (such as appraisals) in line with other more department/team specific processes to maximise performance across the organisation. Blanket policies can only do so much, and although analysing the organisation on an individual by individual basis may be time consuming, it will ultimately lead to a much more rewarding end product for all concerned. As we will see, this framework should act as the starting point of an organic, cyclical performance management process rather than being a permanent, fixed strategy.

This handbook will examine the elements that go into creating a fair and effective performance management strategy, their importance in the strategy and how to go about implementing a strategy as a whole.

It is an ideal tool if you are an employee, employer, volunteer or line manager.

Each individual has a direct responsibility for organisational achievement no matter how large or small the part they play, encouraging them to feel a sense of personal pride at the company's overall success.

The best performance management strategies utilise a number of elements to cover a range of skills and targets and are tailored to departments, teams and individuals of all levels.

The initial framework should act as the starting point of an organic, cyclical performance management process rather than being a permanent, fixed strategy.

Step 1 – The essentials of performance management

Before we embark on putting together a performance management framework, it is important to be aware of how it can be used to help a company at various levels. Performance management is commonly split into four categories. These are as follows.

Organisational performance management

This is where overall strategies and company targets are formulated and plans put in place for the departments involved. Progress towards these goals should be regularly reviewed and altered where necessary rather than just being found to have not been reached at the end of the year. In the public sector where targets are passed down from government the focus is often on working out strategies in order to meet these targets.

Department performance management

Departmental managers receive their targets and performance management strategies through the organisational meetings and subsequently plan out the aims of the teams within their own departments, knowing what each team must achieve in order for the sum of their efforts to produce the stated aim.

Team performance management

Team managers receive their aims from their heads of department and must utilise performance

Performance management is commonly split into four categories:

Organisational performance management *- overall strategies and company targets are formulated and plans put in place for the departments involved.*

Department performance management *- department managers receive their targets and performance management strategies and subsequently plan out the aims of the teams within their own departments.*

Team performance management *- team managers receive their aims and must decide how to utilise performance management to push their team to achieve set goals.*

management strategies in relation to the individuals that make up their team to ensure that the cumulative effort from individuals achieves the group goal.

Individual performance management

Individual performance management ensures that each person in the company is doing their utmost to reach their own personal goal, which will in turn have a bearing on the eventual organisation performance. Ensuring that each individual is aware of the part they play in the entire operation can have a great effect on their levels of motivation. Staff need to feel they are important and valued, and using this style of performance management can show them that each individual represents a crucial link in the overall chain.

This four tier system, and the equivalents that will exist from organisation to organisation, shows how performance management is just as important at an organisational level as it is at an individual one – everybody at all levels needs goals and strategies in place to help them get there. It is also important that the motivation to succeed emanates from the very top of the organisation and cascades downwards.

Your organisation may of course be set up differently to this, but the important thing to bear in mind is that each level within your organisation must be performance managed if the system is to work at all; that way every individual is catered for and no one is

Individual performance management - each individual has their own targets and rewards and is aware of the part they play in the company's success.

Performance management is just as important at an organisational level as it is at an individual one – everybody at all levels needs goals and strategies in place to help them get there.

The motivation to succeed should emanate from the very top of the organisation and cascade downwards.

Each level within your organisation must be performance managed if the system is to work at all.

left out. An individual who is given personal targets alone and does not feel part of the overall company strategy (or if there isn't one in place) may not feel as motivated to perform as someone who is made aware of their importance in the overall plan. This is where managers play an important part – if each manager can get each team member to hit their targets then every brick will fall into place and success on all levels will be achieved. This is also another example of why performance management shouldn't just be reserved for uncovering flaws – trusting in employees and actively helping them through an organic strategy tailored to their individual needs will ensure greater trust, motivation and therefore long-term success than someone who is just picked up for poor performance issues.

Whilst all frameworks will naturally differ from company to company, they should all follow the same general cycle:

An individual who is given personal targets alone and does not feel part of the overall company strategy may not be as motivated to perform as someone who is made aware of their importance in the overall plan.

If each manager can get each team member to hit their targets then every brick will fall into place and success on all levels will be achieved.

Trusting in employees and actively helping them through an organic strategy tailored to their individual needs will ensure greater trust, motivation and long-term success.

Typical management performance cycle

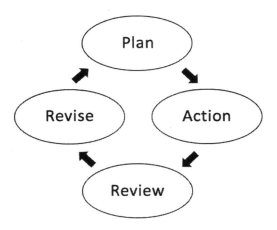

Plan – Targets and aims are outlined, as are the methods of achieving them.

Action – Departments, teams and individuals carry out these new methods for a set period of time.

Review – The strategy is reviewed to check on performance of staff and processes involved.

Revise – Alterations are made to processes where necessary. The cycle begins again.

This cyclical nature is vital to the success of performance management, and once initiated it is a great habit to get into as it prevents organisations from stagnating or 'resting' on short-term peak performance. Many organisations have an HR policy or strategy in place for their staff, and so integrating this with a performance management outlook to create a

Following the performance management cycle prevents organisations from stagnating or resting on short-term peak performance.

fully integrated performance management culture is always recommended. A fully integrated performance management approach requires target setting from the top downwards but also, crucially, the opportunity for all individuals involved to feedback their experiences to influence further change. It is very rare that a new performance management strategy will be an immediate 100% success, and it is crucial that all individuals are given the opportunity to air their thoughts on the strategy and be listened to in order to improve it further.

One final area to note is that performance management doesn't just refer to the performance of the human workforce – it also applies to systems and processes. These include concepts such as Lean and Six Sigma. In a previous book I outlined the benefits of actively searching for ways to increase productivity, including streamlining systems and processes. Again these should not be methods used only when a process becomes flawed but should instead be something that is continually looked at and improvements sought. Everything from implementing new technology to tweaking job responsibilities can improve the speed and efficiency at which a team operates, and striving for better performance should be no different in processes and systems than it is with a workforce.

A fully integrated performance management approach allows for all individuals involved to feedback their experiences to influence further change.

Performance management can also apply to systems and processes as well as a human workforce.

The performance management approach should not be used only when a process becomes flawed but should instead be something that is continually looked at and improvements sought.

"The essence of competitiveness is liberated when we make people believe that what they think and do is important – and then get out of their way while they do it."

Jack Welch, former CEO of GE

"Any organisation which boasts one Statement of Purpose, one Vision, five Values, six Goals, seven Strategic Priorities and eight Key Performance Indicators without any clear correlation between them is producing a recipe for total confusion and exasperation."

Learmont Report on the Prison Service, October 1995

"An empowered organization is one in which individuals have the knowledge, skill, desire, and opportunity to personally succeed in a way that leads to collective organizational success."

Stephen Covey

Step 2 – Goal setting and measuring

Objective or goal setting is, naturally, one of the most important elements of performance management. Success in this area involves marrying an employee's current ability, potential ability and organisational ambitions to find the balance that allows the individual to thrive. Once these goals are set and acted upon, an effective and straightforward method of performance measurement must be implemented in order to track progress towards these goals. We will deal with the measurement aspect in the second half of this section, but the setting of goals will be analysed first.

Successful goal setting involves marrying an employee's current ability, potential ability and organisational ambitions to find the balance that allows the individual to thrive.

Goal setting

The SMART acronym is frequently used when discussing the establishing of goals, and it is one that is relevant in almost all areas of measurable performance. The SMART system advocates that goals should be:

- Specific
- Measurable
- Achievable
- Realistic
- Time based

An effective and straightforward method of performance measurement must be implemented in order to track progress towards these goals.

SMART goals are:

- *Specific*
- *Measurable*
- *Achievable*
- *Realistic*
- *Time based*

To explain this, let's say that a company wants to increase its revenue. The term 'increase revenue' is too vague however and would leave the workforce unsure of exactly what the requirements are. The goal should instead be more specific – i.e. targeting repeat business. For clarity and focus, the goal should also state quantities of improvement – say 25%. This is easily measurable. The target should also be challenging yet within reach, whilst also taking into account other factors such as projected market conditions. This makes the goal both achievable and realistic. Finally, it should be specific to a timescale – within one year, for example. This makes it time based. The original rough aim of increasing revenue has now evolved into a specific, reachable yet challenging target that can be easily measured along the way. If the SMART system is included in goals on every level from organisational down to individual, there is a much greater chance of success given that each employee knows exactly what is required of them.

'Stretch objectives' can also act as useful goal based motivational tools for employees of all levels within an organisation. These are larger objectives that may not necessarily be achievable but are something for organisations, departments and individuals to aspire to in order to move the company onwards to the next level. It may, for example, be a conservatory sales team's objective to increase individual orders from 25 to 30 per month, through which they would earn £5,000 commission each. A stretch objective could also

Specific goals will focus the workforce.

Measurable goals are easier to track in terms of progress.

Achievable and realistic goals will offer greater encouragement to the workforce.

Time based goals offer greater clarity and focus.

The SMART system should be used for goals set at all levels as far as is possible.

Stretch objectives are set purposefully high but, if met, can catapult a business forward.

be set, whereby if they manage 50 per month then they will receive a bonus of £10,000. This objective is not impossible to achieve but is very difficult, which is reflected in the lure of the large bonus. Were each salesperson to meet this stretch objective it would represent a huge boost to the organisation who would see their profits surge and possibly elevate them to major players in the conservatory business. The bonus pays for itself. Stretch objectives therefore are often lower in achievability than other goals but higher in reward.

Stretch objectives can are often lower in achievability but higher in reward.

Performance measurement

Once goals have been established and clearly communicated to staff, they need to be measured. It may be fairly simple in small companies to track progress of goals, but in large organisations, or those with complex goals in place, more detailed methods must be employed. For example, a popular performance measurement tool utilised by modern businesses is the Balanced Scorecard (BSC), which allows an organisation to set out its goals and requirements, quickly and effectively see what progress is being made towards them and detect areas of necessary improvement. The concept was created in 1987 by Arthur Schneiderman as a performance evaluation system but has since seen two revisions which moved it firstly into the management system

Performance measurement is a critical part of the performance management process.

The Balanced Scorecard (BSC) is a commonly used method of measuring performance data.

arena (second generation) and then into its current format as a framework for organisational change (third generation). Appendix I shows the original BSC model.

Whichever incarnation you choose to implement, the principles of the BSC remain the same – it allows quick, convenient and accurate reporting of performance management progress in key areas whilst allowing users to see which parts of the performance management strategy are not working. It also ensures that an organisation doesn't simply focus on sales at the expense of customer service or quality measures – instead it maintains an overall view of numerous aspects contained within its performance management framework. The BSC method is effective because it "articulates the links between leading inputs (human and physical), processes, and lagging outcomes and focuses on the importance of managing these components to achieve the organization's strategic priorities."[1]

The current model has four main components:

- A destination statement. This is a one or two page description of the organisation at a defined point in the future, typically three to five years, assuming the current strategy has been successfully implemented. The descriptions of the successful future are segmented into perspectives, for example

BSC allows quick, convenient and accurate reporting of performance management progress in key areas whilst allowing users to see which parts of the performance management strategy are not working.

The BSC method is effective because it "articulates the links between leading inputs (human and physical), processes, and lagging outcomes and focuses on the importance of managing these components to achieve the organization's strategic priorities."

financial and stakeholder expectations, customer and external relationships, processes and activities and organisation and culture.

- A strategic linkage model. This is a version of the traditional 'strategy map' that typically contains a series of strategic objectives segmented into two perspectives – activities and outcomes.
- A set of definitions for each of the strategic objectives.
- A set of definitions for each of the measures selected to monitor each of the strategic objectives, including targets.

The advantage to this system is that, while external support and training will undoubtedly help in understanding and establishing the process, existing management teams can control and manage all the scorecard content – indeed, it in fact requires active involvement from all managers who will be using the scorecard from the outset.

The BSC method is also useful for creating organisational alignment. Organisational alignment is an essential element of performance management as it ensures that every individual is pulling their weight in the right direction and not skewing the group effort by not fully understanding the goals and strategy set in

The BSC has four components:

- *A destination statement.*

- *A strategic linkage model.*

- *A set of definitions for each of the strategic objectives.*

- *A set of definitions for each of the measures selected to monitor each of the strategic objectives, including targets.*

The BSC requires active involvement from all managers who will be using the scorecard from the outset, and existing management teams can control and manage all the scorecard content.

Organisational alignment is an essential element of performance management.

place. It is vital that organisational alignment begins at the top and is effectively cascaded down the ranks or tiers, starting from tier 1 (organisational) to tier 2 (departments) to tier 3 (teams) and so on until every individual within the remit of the performance management strategy is accounted for. The end result should be a consistent understanding of the strategy across all levels, leaving nobody in any doubt as to what is expected of them as individuals and the company as a whole and ensuring that they recognise the value of their efforts in achieving all the set goals.

A second approach that is rapidly gaining popularity is that of using software to measure performance. From specialist software companies to computer giants like IBM, performance management software is being recognised as the next step in the performance management market. Comprising areas such as employee performance management, corporate performance management, risk management and more. These constantly evolving packages allow for quick, easy and accurate data reporting on all aspects of a performance management strategy. Many performance management practitioners will encourage the use of a software package with their services, but companies can still implement a software based solution exclusively.

Organisational alignment ensures that every individual is pulling their weight in the right direction and not skewing the group effort by not fully understanding the goals and strategy set in place.

It is vital that organisational alignment begins at the top and is effectively cascaded down the organisational ladder.

Computer software is also used to measure performance. Constantly evolving packages allow for quick, easy and accurate data reporting on all aspects of a performance management strategy.

Regular review meetings

A key ingredient in the success of performance measurement, regardless of which system you use, is regular review meetings. When used in tandem with an annual/biannual appraisal (see Step 4), these regular meetings can prove to be incredibly effective in maintaining high performance standards and addressing areas of underperformance swiftly and effectively. A 2009 survey by CIPD supported this idea with respondents, in fact citing regular review meetings as the most important feature of a performance management strategy[2].

When adopting this dual appraisal approach, the job of the annual appraisal is to set out the long-term goals whilst the regular reviews assess performance and track progress towards these goals. This allows underperformance to be detected and tackled long before it becomes a problem, and is easier to achieve with regular statistical data (this goes back to the planning and implementation of the performance management strategy at the outset – if the goal setting procedure was clear and allowed for easy measuring, then this process should be more straightforward). The regular reviews also allow employees to discuss how they are finding the new goals and whether they need anything in the way of training or equipment to enable them to succeed. These meetings are also a good

Regular review meetings are a key ingredient of any performance measurement system.

The job of the annual appraisal is to set out the long-term goals whilst the regular reviews assess performance and track progress towards these goals.

Regular meetings allow underperformance to be detected and tackled long before it becomes a problem.

The regular reviews also allow employees to discuss how they are finding the new goals and whether they need anything else to enable them to succeed.

chance to reinforce employee engagement (see Step 5) and show the employee how the company is faring in its organisational goals.

Regular reviews will ideally occur every four to six weeks. They tend to be less structured than formal appraisals, although naturally the same professional standards should be upheld. They shouldn't be long, drawn out affairs (around 30 to 60 minutes is ideal) and should consist of items which either party wish to raise in the context of the employee's role, performance or development. The role of the line manager (or managers where a matrix structure exists) is critical. He or she must be adequately equipped to conduct the appraisal discussion; it is not about form filling and box ticking but having a quality discussion (see Step 4 for more details). The focus of the discussion should centre around:

- The general performance of the employee, as it relates to their job description and the associated standard of performance.
- Progress made towards previously agreed personal objectives, whether performance-related or developmental.
- Progress towards objectives within the employee's personal improvement plan (see Step 7) or in meeting other training needs as they arise.

Regular reviews will ideally occur every four to six weeks and should consist of items which either party wish to raise in the context of the employee's role, performance or development.

The manager(s) responsible for the review meetings must be adequately equipped to conduct the appraisal; it is not about form filling and box ticking but having a quality discussion.

The discussion should centre around:

- *The general performance of the employee.*
- *Progress made towards previously agreed personal objectives.*
- *Progress towards objectives within the employee's personal improvement plan (if set).*

The attitude and approach to these regular reviews should be in line with that of the larger appraisals. One of the advantages of regular reviews is the opportunity to spot potential performance issues sooner than those utilising annual appraisals alone. These opportunities should not be wasted, as they sometimes are by line managers who neglect to tackle such issues early on. Acting on warning signs rather than fully developed performance slumps is preferable for many reasons, so ensure that all line managers are fully equipped and able to recognise and deal with issues at this early stage (see Step 8 for more information). As with all appraisal related meetings, employees should leave the meeting motivated to perform. They should feel that their efforts will bring the rewards that drive them personally and that they are part of the organisation's success. Dates for following meetings should be either agreed at the end of each meeting or set out in advance for a longer period so the employee is focused and knows when they will next be reviewed.

Opportunities to address poor performance early on should always be taken.

Employees should leave the meeting motivated to perform and assured that they are part of the organisation's success.

"There is a surprising degree of agreement that performance appraisal, objective setting, regular feedback, regular reviews and assessment of development needs are the cornerstones of performance management."

CIPD

"Good leadership consists of showing average people how to do the work of superior people."

John D. Rockerfeller

"Measurement is the first step that leads to control and eventually to improvement. If you can't measure something, you can't understand it. If you can't understand it, you can't control it. If you can't control it, you can't improve it."

H. James Harrington

Step 3 – Reward strategies

Rewarding performance is a complex area, especially in a performance management setting. To get the best out of a performance management strategy, reward strategies have to be individualised and constantly reviewed, whilst managers themselves need to work out what makes each employee in their team tick and create a tailored reward system based on these differences of character. This method requires an insightful manager who cares greatly about getting the best from his or her staff and employees who desire challenges and targets. This combination, if found, can produce a highly efficient team.

Reward strategies should be individualised and constantly reviewed for maximum effect.

An insightful manager who wants to get the best out of their team and employees who like being challenged are the ideal combination.

Whilst studies show that financial rewards are actually decreasing in importance to employees, pay and bonuses are, and will continue to be, the most common and recognised forms of reward. Whilst higher pay doesn't necessarily go hand in hand with higher motivation, there is no doubt that the majority of employees will respond well to a salary and bonus based reward scheme. Managing a fair yet fluctuating pay management scheme is a challenging process. Equality is vital however, not necessarily in terms of pay itself but the scale of achievement to reward. 'Regular' team members will generally have no issue with high achievers earning more than them. In fact it will be almost expected, but those who are rewarded

Financial rewards may be decreasing in importance to employees, but pay and bonuses are, and will continue to be, the most common and recognised forms of reward.

to the same or even a higher value for what others perceive as lesser targets can result in resentment. This is where targets of different natures can be a blessing and a curse – different people will see different rewards in different ways.

Broadly speaking there are two camps that rewards fall into – extrinsic and intrinsic. The following is a breakdown of what these terms mean and what kind of rewards fit into these categories.

Extrinsic

Extrinsic rewards are those that involve some external motivation on behalf of the employee, for example money, status and power. Extrinsic motivation almost uses the method of attainment as a stepping stone to the goal, whereas an intrinsic motivation is one which derives satisfaction from the attainment method itself. Extrinsic rewards often take the form of a salary increase or bonus, time off, improved work environment or conditions (new car, bigger office, etc.), promotion or more job security. An employee who is largely or solely extrinsically motivated usually has further ambitions for the rewards they seek – maybe they are saving for a house, car or holiday or they simply want to keep up with or exceed their contemporaries.

'Regular' team members will generally have no issue with high achievers earning more than them, but be careful to ensure that performance and reward are proportionate across the board.

Extrinsic rewards are those that involve some external motivation on behalf of the employee, for example money, status and power.

Extrinsic motivation almost uses the method of attainment as a stepping stone to the goal.

Intrinsic

Intrinsic rewards are based around personal fulfilment, job satisfaction and the knowledge of contribution to overall success of the individual. Intrinsic rewards are often harder to put in place as they depend hugely on the nature of the individual and what motivates them. Of course all of us are driven by money to a certain extent, but for many, once they are earning over a comfortable amount, then job satisfaction and personal fulfilment becomes the priority. The realisation that not everyone is driven by financial rewards explains why early adopters of performance management strategies, which were more or less wholly extrinsically based, were not overly successful. To help understand intrinsic motivations, Kenneth Thomas of the Ivy Business Journal uncovered four common values which managers can base their intrinsic rewards around. These are:

- Sense of **meaningfulness**. This reward involves the meaningfulness or importance of the purpose you are trying to fulfil. You feel that you have an opportunity to accomplish something of real value—something that matters in the larger scheme of things. You feel that you are on a path that is worth your time and energy, giving you a strong sense of purpose or direction.

Intrinsic rewards are based around personal fulfilment, job satisfaction and the knowledge of contribution to overall success of the individual.

Four common values for intrinsic rewards have been identified:

Sense of meaningfulness *- you feel that you are on a path that is worth your time and energy, giving you a strong sense of purpose or direction.*

- Sense of **choice**. You feel free to choose how to accomplish your work, to use your best judgment to select those work activities that make the most sense to you and to perform them in ways that seem appropriate. You feel ownership of your work, believe in the approach you are taking, and feel responsible for making it work.

  Sense of choice - you feel ownership of your work, believe in the approach you are taking, and feel responsible for making it work.

- Sense of **competence**. You feel that you are handling your work activities well—that your performance of these activities meets or exceeds your personal standards, and that you are doing good, high quality work. You feel a sense of satisfaction, pride, or even artistry in how well you handle these activities.

  Sense of competence - you feel a sense of satisfaction, pride, or even artistry in how well you handle daily activities.

- Sense of **progress**. You are encouraged that your efforts are really accomplishing something. You feel that your work is on track and moving in the right direction. You see convincing signs that things are working out, giving you confidence in the choices you have made and confidence in the future.[3]

  Sense of progress - you see convincing signs that things are working out, giving you confidence in the choices you have made and confidence in the future.

Of course not all employees will value all of these things, and most of us carry a combination of extrinsic and intrinsic values, but for more intrinsically motivated staff these ideals represent a good starting point for a manager lacking experience in intrinsic

Most of us carry a mix of extrinsic and intrinsic motivations.

motivation skills. Examples of intrinsic motivations can include further recognition/awards, further training/personal development, higher profile projects and equipment to do their jobs better.

Where possible, rewards should not only match the personal ambitions of the employee, but they should also be relative to the others in their team. Dealing with intrinsically and extrinsically motivated people within the same team is a huge challenge for a line manager, given the raft of rewards that could potentially be offered, but as far as possible equality should be maintained where employees are of equal stature in the company.

In the best performance management strategies, employees should help come up with their own rewards rather than being told what they are. This way the employee has a stake in their own success and will be more motivated to achieve something they genuinely want rather than something their line manager thinks they want. Line managers should also not be afraid to ask what their employees want as a reward. It is a simple way to know if they are generally extrinsically or intrinsically motivated and compromises may be able to be reached.

The reward scheme for underperformers is naturally a little different. Offering the same type of reward for effectively less work will not go down well with the rest of the team.

When it comes to dealing with rewards for underperformers, the situation will naturally be a little different. Generally in these situations a manager will be seeking to get the employee up to the standard of others rather than trying to push them to excel, and so offering the same type of reward for effectively less work will not go down well with the rest of the team. In situations where underperformance is an issue, a manager needs to recognise the steps that need to be taken to get the employee to a satisfactory standard, including any issues with training, ability and equipment etc. Once these areas have been assessed, underperforming employees must be given a reward structure to ensure that they are motivated enough to want to get to the requisite level. Targets should also be reviewed and amended as performance changes – poor performers for example may need different kinds of targets and support to get them to the same level as others.

As well as individual reward programmes, team reward programmes can also be implemented in order to further spur performance. However, seeing as this type of reward system doesn't take into account individual effort, only team performance as a whole, some harder workers may feel a little put out that their less hard working colleagues share in their success.

Differences also occur in reward strategies in the public and private sectors. Private sector employees typically receive a higher base salary but a lower (or no) contribution to a company pension. Short-term, cash

Managers need to recognise the steps that need to be taken to get the employee to a satisfactory standard and then implement a fair reward system.

Targets should be reviewed and amended as performance changes.

Team reward programmes can also be very effective, although some harder workers may feel a little put out if their less hard working colleagues share in their success

based bonus and incentive schemes are widespread in this sector, whereas those in the public sector have far less access to such targeted and structured reward systems. With budgets typically tighter in this sector, rewards such as extra holiday, flexible working patterns and training and development are more common, although steps have been made in recent years to try and address this imbalance.

Private sector employees typically receive a higher base salary but a lower (or no) contribution to a company pension, whereas those in the public sector are often rewarded with extra holiday, flexible working patterns and training and development.

With all this in mind, the following are a number of important points to bear in mind whilst considering your reward strategy:

- Performance must be capable of being measured and tracked throughout the period over which the performance is being assessed. It should therefore be clear and easily understood by all employees.

- There must be a clear link between effort and reward.

- The reward should be worthwhile and attainable, although not too easily achieved.

- Good pay has not been shown to equal good performance. However, poor pay has been shown to demotivate.

- High levels of pay on their own do not generally result in high performance levels.

- All individual objectives should contribute towards achieving the organisations defined goals.

- Reward structures have been known to skew performance towards short-term rather than long-term focus. This side effect is the subject of an ongoing debate within performance management circles, but it is something to certainly be wary of.

"Do not hire a man who does your work for money, but him who does it for love of it."

Henry David Thoreau

"The only man I know who behaves sensibly is my tailor; he takes my measurements anew each time he sees me. The rest go on with their old measurements and expect me to fit them"

George Bernard Shaw

"Always recognize that human individuals are ends, and do not use them as means to your end."

Immanuel Kant

Step 4 – The appraisal

As previously mentioned, the appraisal system is used by many organisations as the sole performance management strategy, thus placing huge emphasis on its outcome and therefore more pressure on the person conducting it. Within a performance management strategy however the appraisal runs alongside regular reviews (see Step 2) and is used to analyse performance over a longer period (usually six months or a year), set long-term goals and attribute rewards as appropriate. Appraisals are also a chance for employees to discuss their thoughts on their job, the company and any wider concerns or ideas they may have and they should be completely confident that their thoughts will remain confidential and be acted on where appropriate. If the company has an employee engagement programme in place (see Step 5) then an appraisal is also a great chance to renew or strengthen employee/company ties and reinforce the employee's importance within the company.

When used as part of a performance management strategy an appraisal takes on a different significance, requiring a variety of skills from those giving the appraisal. Appraisal givers are often line managers rather than trained HR professionals which can present problems, but problems that can be overcome if the right approach is adopted from the outset and the

Within a performance management strategy the appraisal runs alongside regular reviews and is used to analyse performance over a longer period (usually six months or a year).

Appraisals are also a chance for employees to discuss their thoughts on their job, the company and any wider concerns or ideas they may have.

When used as part of a performance management strategy an appraisal takes on a different significance, requiring a variety of skills from those giving the appraisal.

framework in place is sufficient. A quality discussion is much more important than the appraisal documentation.

A major difference between a standard appraisal and one as part of a performance management strategy is that the former tends to be an annual review, taking into account everything that has happened in a set period, usually the last 12 months but more commonly the last six. While this is technically the same for the latter, the appraisal should take into account all the regular review meetings that have occurred during the period and so should be more of a summing up of overall performance rather than a 'first look' at what has happened over the course of the appraisal period. There should therefore be no surprises if regular review meetings have been taking place.

A traditional appraisal tends to be an annual review, whilst an appraisal as part of a performance management strategy should take in all the regular review meetings that have taken place.

The ideal appraisal framework should be structured so that all points can be addressed whilst allowing flexibility within that structure so that matters can be discussed fully on both sides. Appraisal templates should follow the same format company wide but should be departmentally tailored to reflect the different work, responsibilities and targets required by different departments. Regardless of the format, they should all follow a similar framework. A typical framework will allow for the following:

Ideally, appraisals will be structured in order that set areas can be addressed but flexible enough to encourage more general topics of work discussion.

- An introduction stating the purpose of the appraisal.

- A review of the objectives set at the last appraisal and a discussion as to whether they have been met or otherwise. If the objectives have not been met, reasons for failure should be discussed, solutions found and help offered where necessary.

- If required, a personal improvement plan should be discussed and set down (see Step 7).

- The employee should be given sufficient time to discuss any concerns they have about their work or the company.

- A reminder of the employee's importance to the company and their responsibilities towards overall success as part of an employee engagement programme.

- The next year's objectives should be agreed and set, as well as regular review dates. Any training and development required by the employee to meet these objectives should also be discussed.

Before the emergence of performance management as a mainstream strategy, much importance was attached to the annual appraisal. Whilst it is still an important part of a performance management strategy it no longer holds as much significance and so shouldn't act as the first and last word in performance measurement and salary/bonus planning. A good appraisal in this setting will take into account the other aspects of the performance management strategy and will use the appraisal to bring them together to reach a final conclusion.

There can be a tendency to assume too much from an appraisal exercise, but the individual being appraised will expect the following outcomes from their appraisal:

- Receive constructive feedback on all aspects of their performance.
- Be made aware what their career prospects are for the period and in the future.
- Be able to air grievances about management or the organisation without it affecting their prospects.
- Be able to discuss salary frankly.
- Understand what their objectives are for the period ahead.
- Above all, to feel notice has been taken of what they have said.

In an ideal world an employee will leave their appraisal in good spirits having had their importance to the company asserted, their motivation boosted and the knowledge that, with hard work and application, their

The annual/bi-annual appraisal shouldn't act as the first and last word in performance measurement and salary/bonus planning.

prospects at the company are bright. Of course this can't always happen, but a tactfully handled appraisal can incorporate many if not all of the elements mentioned here and leave the employee in an upbeat and positive mood. Some managers feel uncomfortable giving appraisals, especially when negative conversations are likely to be involved. This area is tackled in more detail in Step 8, but the following notes will help managers prepare for an appraisal whatever the anticipated outcome.

A tactfully handled appraisal can leave the employee in an upbeat and positive mood, even if the conversation is not positive in nature.

The first stage of the appraisal is to complete your written assessment of the employee's performance. Before beginning, set a mutually convenient date, time and location for the appraisal which allows adequate preparation time for both you and the employee. This done, gather the following materials:

Set a mutually convenient date, time and location for the appraisal and gather the relevant materials for the written assessment.

- The employee's job description and performance standards.
- The previous performance appraisal, especially goals set.
- Performance data for the period in relation to set goals.
- Work rules and procedures.
- External or internal feedback about the employee.

Using this information, first make notes on the following areas before committing them to the form:

- The main areas of responsibility.
- The employee's level of success in reaching their set goals for the period.
- What the employee has done well.
- What the employee needs to improve on.
- What you can do to help the employee do a better job.
- How the employee's input affects the performance of the team, department and company in line with the company's employee engagement policy.

This done, review the notes and ensure that, as much as possible, a balanced view of the employee is offered. Transfer these notes to the appraisal form, ensuring where possible to end on positive points. If the employee is required to write a self appraisal, be sure to obtain this early enough so you have a chance to review it (if this is the case, be sure too to provide the employee with a draft of your appraisal for similar purposes).

Different people will tackle appraisals in different ways, but there are some key things that every appraisal giver should bear in mind. Firstly, remember that you want the employee to leave the appraisal motivated despite a possible discussion of poor performance

Review the notes and ensure that, as much as possible, a balanced view of the employee is offered.

Leave plenty of time for the employee to read your appraisal and to read theirs if they have one.

Be fair and reasonable in your assessment of their performance and display trust and faith in their ability to turn a bad situation round.

having taken place. To this end you need to appear fair and reasonable in your assessment of their performance and display trust and faith in their ability to turn a bad situation round. Ideally the employee should also leave the meeting assured of their importance in the overall company performance, in line with the company's employee engagement policy if one is implemented. Ensure that you illustrate to them just how important their individual performance is to the overall performance of the company and how valued they are.

Ensure that you reinforce how important the employee's individual performance is to the overall performance of the company and how valued they are.

If there is one key thing to remember about the way to handle an appraisal it is that many employees rate trust in their line manager as the most important factor in work motivation. If you are demonstrably fair in your evaluation of their performance, if you set fair yet challenging goals and you pledge to support them in reaching those goals then you can be confident that you have done all you can to help them succeed.

Many employees rate trust in their line manager as the most important factor in work motivation, so fairness and support are key aspects of all appraisals.

"The single biggest problem in communication is the illusion that it has taken place."

George Bernard Shaw

"How you measure the performance of your managers directly affects the way they act."

John Dearden

"Fairness is not an attitude. It's a professional skill that must be developed and exercised."

Brit Hume

Step 5 – Performance management and employee engagement

Employee engagement as a term was first coined as late as 1993, but the concept behind it is based on the long established idea of job satisfaction – how engaging our jobs are, how happy we are with them and whether we feel like a valued member of the team or just another number on the payroll. In keeping with its relatively recent inception, the idea of multilevel job satisfaction and its importance in the modern workforce is something that employers have only recently sought to maximise. Many are however beginning to realise that a happy, engaged workforce is a productive one, and that, as I outlined in Step 2, different factors drive different people, meaning ever more creative methods of engagement have to be sought.

Ideally an employee engagement strategy will run in tandem with a performance management strategy, but there is no harm in implementing an employee engagement programme on its own if you feel it is what your business is missing. Increasing the connection your employees feel with an organisation should fuel better performance regardless, and a performance management strategy can always follow afterwards. In short, if you can't have both then it is better to have an employee engagement strategy and

Employee engagement refers to how engaging our jobs are, how happy we are with them and whether we feel like a valued member of the team or just another number on the payroll.

Different factors drive different people, meaning ever more creative methods of engagement have to be sought to keep a workforce content and productive.

Increasing the connection your employees feel with an organisation should fuel better performance, and a performance management strategy can always follow afterwards.

no performance management strategy than the other way round. Employee engagement is crucial to the success of a performance management strategy as everyone needs to buy into it and believe in it to make it work, and an unengaged workforce is much less likely to do that.

To answer the question of why employee engagement is important, consider the reverse situation – how would a company perform if its employees were unmotivated, bored and ill-rewarded? It doesn't take an industry expert to see that problems will soon arise, but this is the risk companies run when they don't focus on how their employees feel about their jobs (signs of low employee engagement include high absenteeism, high staff turnover, decreased productivity and more disciplinary issues). Engaged employees on the other hand are far more conscientious about the work they do, care about the future of the company and are more willing to invest discretionary effort[4].

Employee engagement is also a reflection of what individuals get back from their jobs and how adequately it satisfies them. This level of satisfaction will naturally vary from person to person and will include everything from colleagues to environment to the work they do. This may seem an unruly thing to try and control, but the truth is that companies can

Employee engagement is crucial to the success of a performance management strategy as everyone needs to buy into it and believe in it to make it work.

Companies who disregard their employee's happiness and welfare may find themselves suffering high absenteeism, high staff turnover, decreased productivity and more disciplinary issues.

Workforce happiness may seem an unruly thing to try and control, but the truth is that companies can control and influence these aspects more to create a harmonious and productive workforce, even on a small budget.

control and influence these aspects more to create a harmonious and productive workforce, even on a small budget.

Before planning an employee engagement programme, it is important to consider what factors drive employee engagement. The four most relevant are listed below.

Trust

Trust is one of the most important and powerful characteristics a manager can bestow upon his or her team. A manager who can demonstrate selflessness and foster trust will find that the team will be more motivated and will do more to rectify mistakes and achieve results. Almost everyone can remember a manager they enjoyed working for, and the chances are that one of the primary reasons was trust – we had faith that they would lead the team in the right direction and we would support them to the hilt in order to do that. Economic downturns provide stern tests of the employee/manager relationship, given that line managers are responsible for delivering news of redundancies and the like. However, as long as such redundancies are seen to be fair and well handled, as all employment terminations should be, that bond of trust should be easier to repair than with a manager who dismisses indiscriminately and without compassion. Interestingly, studies in this area frequently show that employee trust in direct

A manager who can demonstrate selflessness and foster trust will find that the team will be more motivated and will do more to rectify mistakes and achieve results.

Economic downturns can strain trust in a manager, but as long as the manager shows themself to be fair and handles any redundancies professionally then the bond will be repaired easier.

managers is vastly higher than trust in more senior managers.

Learning and development

In order to create a motivated and engaged workforce, employees need to feel that the company is not just supporting the work they are doing at that moment but is actively supporting their development, both personal and career wise. They need to know that the organisation is interested in helping them expand their skill set and will assist in helping them broaden their life experience (fashion house Reiss actively recruit from the shop floor, whilst Burberry allow staff extra paid leave to assist in charity work around the world). Learning and development is a key factor in staff retention, whilst taking the time to find and develop individuals rather than recruiting fresh for every position has numerous bonuses.

Employees like to feel that their organisation cares about their development, both career wise and personally.

Training internal staff has numerous benefits over recruiting externally.

Meaningful and engaging work

Some industries have obvious purpose and meaning attached to them (teaching, healthcare etc.), but many of us need other sources of worth to motivate us and keep us engaged in our jobs. This is where a clear and effective performance management strategy can help. If a clear line of sight exists between the tasks an individual performs and the organisation's goals then there is a reason to perform these tasks to the highest

Employees need to attach meaning to their work in order to care about it and perform it well.

standard. If however an employee finds themselves frequently performing tasks that have little or no impact on the performance of the organisation then their engagement with their job will naturally suffer. Streamlining of systems and processes can help cut out meaningless meetings, conference calls and emails and leave only the most important tasks to be done. As well as being meaningful, the work itself should not be dull and boring – or rather it should not be made boring by inefficiency and lack of direction. Work that is not stimulating means lower staff satisfaction, higher turnover and more mistakes as employees aren't as interested in their jobs.

Meaning can sometimes come with the job, but if not then their work needs to be seen to have an impact in overall success.

Work that is not stimulating means lower staff satisfaction, higher turnover and more mistakes.

Fair and fulfilling reward

Given that we devote so much of our lives to work, we quite rightly expect to be adequately rewarded. This comes chiefly in the form of remuneration, but recent research has shown that employees no longer feel that financial rewards on their own are enough to provide high levels of engagement. Instead, appreciation is creeping up the tables of employee satisfaction. A recent study by found that appreciation when run in tandem with the four engagement factors mentioned here can significantly improve employee engagement[5].The best kind of appreciation is that which is unexpected but deserved, rather than anything established and therefore expected as part of

Appreciation for the work we do does more for engagement than a large salary, yet many managers don't praise their staff enough.

Unexpected but deserved praise is the most effective for boosting staff morale and engagement.

a performance management strategy. We all know how good it feels to be praised for something we've done, and this simple act of taking the time to congratulate someone for a well completed task can do more for employee engagement than a four figure pay rise.

Whilst there are no silver bullets when it comes to methods of implementing employee engagement, the key thing to remember is that some workforces and trade unions can be a cynical bunch, and it is a possibility that they will view an employee engagement strategy as a method of increasing discretionary effort only. These doubts haven't been helped by reports of poorly implemented performance management plans that increase workload and stress, which is why it is important to consult trade unions from the outset and ensure that they understand your plans and reasoning, for their support may prove to be invaluable. Any reasonable trade union leader should see that employment engagement is designed to benefit their members as well as the management and that it will help strengthen bonds between the two camps over time.

Some trade unions can be a cynical bunch and may see an employee engagement strategy as a backhanded way to increase discretionary output.

Involve union leaders from the outset. Take their thoughts on board and keep them in the loop – they could prove to be a vital ally.

"If you pick the right people and give them the opportunity to spread their wings—and put compensation as a carrier behind it—you almost don't have to manage them."

Jack Welch

"The conventional definition of management is getting work done through people, but real management is developing people through work."

Agha Hasan Abedi

"Trust men and they will be true to you; treat them greatly and they will show themselves great."

Ralph Waldo Emerson

Step 6 – Performance management and talent management

Talent management represents the policies and systems in place for recruiting, retaining and developing top talent in order to boost organisation performance. It is no secret that talented, driven employees are key to organisational success, and many businesses have realised that investing in this area is more key than any other.

Defining talent management is not as easy as it may seem, for the reason that defining 'talent' itself is difficult. There are varying views on what qualifies as talent in a workplace context, but the CIPD offers the following definition:

Talent consists of those individuals who can make a difference to organisational performance either through their immediate contribution or, in the longer-term, by demonstrating the highest levels of potential.

They also define talent management as the following:

Talent management is the systematic attraction, identification, development, engagement, retention and deployment of those individuals who are of particular value to an organisation, either in view of their 'high potential' for the future or because they are fulfilling business/operation-critical roles.[5]

Talent management represents the policies and systems in place for recruiting, retaining and developing top talent.

'Talent' is defined by the CIPD as "...those individuals who make a difference to organisational performance..."

The CIPD defines talent management as "...the systematic attraction, identification, development, engagement, retention and deployment of those individuals who are of particular value to an organisation..."

Talent management and the 'war for talent' therefore is one of the most important areas in the whole performance management spectrum as a successful strategy can be the difference between average performance and great performance – the same tools in the hands of good people and average people will yield different results. Very few organisations, if any, can boast exceptional staff in all positions, and while this may be a pipe dream, an effective talent management strategy as part of a performance management strategy will undoubtedly make a huge difference.

A successful talent management strategy can be the difference between average performance and great performance.

Talent management is often referred to as an internal or in-house process, but it can be used as a powerful external tool too. Not only does identifying, developing and promoting talent internally have benefits such as reduced recruitment costs, higher staff retention, higher staff satisfaction and strengthened brand identity, it also attracts a higher calibre of external candidate who may be aware that internal promotion is a feature of the business. Many of the facets that make up internal talent management therefore have knock on effects to external talent management too.

An effective talent management strategy as part of a performance management strategy will undoubtedly have a huge impact on business growth and performance.

Talent management can be used externally too.

One of the fundamentals to keep in mind when designing and implementing a talent management strategy is that it must be aligned to the corporate strategy. The reasons for this are clear – if the two

A strong talent management strategy will attract a higher calibre of external candidate.

don't tie in then there is a high probability that the individuals required to fulfil the corporate strategy won't be developed internally or hired externally through the talent management strategy. The solution to this lies in the planning stages of performance management, where important questions are asked such as 'what is the direction of the company?', 'what are the long-term targets?' and 'what sort of company do we want to be?' From here you can start to ask questions such as 'what sort of people are going to get us there?' which will lead you to more specific agendas like what skills and attributes can be classified as vital, preferable and undesirable when it comes to candidate selection, both internal and external.

Important questions must be asked when planning a performance management strategy:

- *What is the direction of the company?*
- *What are the long-term targets?*
- *What sort of company do we want to be?*
- *What sort of people are going to get us there?*

Identifying and developing top performers

Once you know what you are looking for, the next step is trying to identify the top performers and future stars. Internally, a good performance management strategy and a clear knowledge of sought after skills cascaded down the organisation should render this a largely straightforward task. Line managers who are in tune with their team may also be able to offer more in-depth analysis on individuals as well as spotting employees who have skills that could be better utilised in other areas (finding managers who can spot these attributes could form part of your company aims). This process is generally much easier with external

A good performance management strategy and a clear knowledge of sought after skills should render talent spotting much easier.

Attuned line managers may also spot potential talent in their team.

candidates, as they should be trying hard to display as many of their skills as possible. A rigorous interview process should also help identify any useful hidden talents.

Once these individuals have been identified, it is important to plant the seed of potential development early on. This can be a delicate matter, especially if the individual hasn't yet given much thought to their future, and it is therefore important to test the waters quickly before planning their future for them. Some driven and focused individuals may be eager to hear what they can achieve with the company, and it is important here to ensure that, as far as possible, the individual knows that their ambitions can be matched and suitably rewarded by the company. Illustrating the successes of other internally promoted individuals can help offer real life examples of what can be achieved. This process should be mirrored at interview stage with external candidates.

With plans in place for identifying talent, the next step is to develop and manage it effectively. There are various schools of thought on this subject, and strategies are often tailored to individual companies and employees. One thing that is agreed upon across the board is that talent management is one of the very few areas in business where investment should be prioritised; products, price cuts and future intentions

Once potential future stars have been identified, it is important to plant the seed of development.

Don't push them into anything or you may push them away, but ensure they are aware of what they may be able to achieve with your company.

Illustrating the successes of other internally promoted individuals can help offer real life examples of what can be achieved.

Talent management is an area of business where investment should be prioritised, even in economic downturns.

can be imitated by competitors, but imitating a strong, engaged workforce is almost impossible.

Retaining top talent

Whilst it isn't possible to delve into the finer details of the various talent management strategies out there, in this short book we can look at some of the recognised means of developing and retaining top talent. If you are considering implementing the steps already outlined in this book then much of the groundwork will already be in place – reward strategies, employee engagement and effective goal setting all help retain performers of all levels – but even if you are not considering all the options then the golden rule to remember about retaining top performers is 'communication'.

The importance of regular communication with employees of all levels is alluded to in Steps 2, 3 and 5, but regularly discussing top performers' job satisfaction and, most importantly, their future plans should ensure that their superiors have a full understanding of the mindset their top performers are in and can act accordingly to engage, challenge and reward them appropriately. Fostering strong relationships with top performers creates a bond between the individual and the company that can ward off many competitors. This has the added advantage that your company and brand becomes synonymous

Reward strategies, employee engagement and effective goal setting all help retain performers of all levels, but retaining the services of the brightest stars may require more.

The golden rule to remember about retaining top performers is 'communication'.

Regularly discussing top performers' job satisfaction and, most importantly, their future plans should ensure that their superiors have a full understanding of the mindset of their top performers.

Fostering strong relationships with top performers creates a bond between the individual and the company that can ward off many competitors.

with retaining and developing top talent, whilst the individuals themselves enjoy working for the company, something that will only help attract top performers in the future.

If you feel that your top performers are unsure of exactly how they will fit in with the company going forward, it may be wise to consider tailoring a position for them – a post that, as long as it is in line with the corporate strategy, utilises their strongest skills in order to drive the company forward. You may wish to go one step further and illustrate that you plan to shape certain aspects of the company around them in the future, thus ensuring that they are a key part of the company's plans.

Consider tailoring a position for a top performer, or building a team around them.

Top performers often enjoy being challenged and pushed to new heights, which is where regular reviews can be a great help – that way line managers can accurately keep track of performance and ensure that their goals are testing enough or, at the other end of the scale, being met. Flexibility is a key tool to employ when dealing with top performers – you could find yourself needing to discuss role expansion, promotion or new goals and reward strategies at a moment's notice. It is important however to remember that all this must be done with discretion and fairness, as mentioned in Step 3.

Top performers enjoy being challenged. Use regular review meetings to reassess targets throughout the year.

Flexibility is a key attribute when it comes to dealing with top performers. Managers need to be quick on their feet to ensure that their stars are happy in the present and their needs will be met in the future.

Key areas

Given the nature of talent management there aren't any one-size-fits-all solutions to retaining top performers, but there are some areas to pay particular attention to. The CIPD have identified "coaching, mentoring and networking" as highly rated aspects of talent management programmes, as well as "the opportunity to meet senior people in the organisation"[7].

Coaching, mentoring and networking have been identified as highly rated aspects of talent management programmes.

A mistake companies often make when trying to retain and engage a top performer is to spread them too thin or to use their skills incorrectly. It is important to give top performers the responsibility they need to thrive, but restraint must be used in terms of how they are deployed. A square peg, no matter how talented, will not fit into a round hole, and there will be plenty of other organisations who will be able to identify and utilise these individuals' strongest suits.

"Top talent can get competitive pay and benefits at many companies. Employers must earn the loyalty and discretionary effort of their best people."

It is important to give top performers the responsibility they need to thrive, but restraint must be used in terms of how they are deployed.

It is very difficult to find many 'one-size-fits-all' talent management strategies for the reasons discussed, and there really is no substitute for sitting down with your top performers and discussing what they need from you in order for them, and therefore you, to thrive. When it comes to developing and nurturing top performers, it is often the case that those responsible for the task will need to allocate more time and resources than with other employees, but this echoes

There really is no substitute for sitting down with your top performers and discussing what they need from you in order for them to thrive.

the sentiment that commitment to the talent management cause is always a commitment worth making. The war for talent will always be fierce, and it is important to know how to retain and develop game changers when you see them.

Those responsible for retaining and developing key individuals will need to allocate more time and resources than with other employees, but it is very much worth doing.

"Hire people who are better than you are, then leave them to get on with it. Look for people who will aim for the remarkable, who will not settle for the routine."

David Ogilvy

"The art of choosing men is not nearly so difficult as the art of enabling those one has chosen to attain their full worth."

Napoleon Bonaparte

"I believe the real difference between success and failure in a corporation can be very often traced to the question of how well the organization brings out the great energies and talents of its people."

Thomas J. Watson

Step 7 – Performance improvement plans

One of the advantages of a well implemented performance management strategy is that detecting areas of underperformance should be relatively straightforward providing an adequate performance measurement tool has been implemented alongside it. Using such a tool, areas of underperformance should be easily identified, from which action can be taken to remedy the problems found. With some employees a quick conversation about their performance and capability could be sufficient to improve their performance, but on occasions further formal action needs to be taken. This is where performance improvement plans (PIPs) come into play. Treating everyone with dignity and respect is a good principle to bear in mind early on in this chapter.

PIPs are essentially agreements drawn up by underperforming individuals and their managers that clearly set out areas of required improvement using specific targets and time frames, ideally implementing the SMART method of goal setting (see Step 2), with equally clear consequences for failure. By laying out guidelines in this manner, employees are left under no illusions about what is required and are fully aware of just how much responsibility lies with them. A successful PIP enables a manager to set goals, measure

A well implemented performance management strategy should allow easy detection of underperformance.

Some employees may respond positively just by knowing they are being monitored, but some need more formal steps in order to improve.

Performance improvement plans (PIPs) are agreements drawn up by underperforming individuals and their managers that clearly set out areas of required improvement.

By laying out guidelines in this manner, employees are left under no illusions about what is required and are fully aware of just how much responsibility lies with them.

success, conduct review sessions, and chart the progress of that employee.

Formal PIPs will naturally vary depending on a wide variety of factors, but the process generally follows this path:

Determination of underperformance: Under-performance is detected using the chosen performance measurement tool.

PIP intention notice issued: The employee is notified of his or her underperformance and is informed that a PIP will be implemented.

PIP implemented: A PIP is drawn up and the employee is made aware of required improvements and consequences of continued underperformance.

Determination of improvement: Employee performance is monitored for change in line with agreed targets and timelines and relevant action taken if improvement is not satisfactory.

There are a number of important factors to consider when planning an employee PIP. The first is to identify specifically which areas of performance are lacking – the more specific the better. If you can use data from your performance measurement tool to illustrate statistical data then it is best to do so. Next, take each area of underperformance and indicate the standards to which the employee should be adhering. Ensure too

The PIP process generally follows this path:

- *Determination of underperformance.*

- *PIP intention notice issued.*

- *PIP implemented.*

- *Determination of improvement.*

Identify specifically which areas of performance are lacking – the more specific the better.

Take each area of underperformance and indicate the standards to which the employee should be adhering.

Ensure that the employee realises that these performance levels must be consistent.

that the employee realises that these performance levels must be consistent, as employees on PIPs are known to improve for a short time and then fade back to their previous standards after a while. As we have already seen, allowing the employee to assist in deciding on goals and targets may bring better rewards as they feel they have more of a stake in their own performance. Ask them also if they feel they need any extra assistance in performing their duties. You may discover that there are underlying reasons for the underperformance such as ill health or personal issues. These may trigger further HR processes, so be prepared for potentially escalating the case as required.

Once the plan itself has been agreed, inform the employee of the repercussions of failing to meet the requirements of the PIP and ensure that they are fully aware of the ramifications of doing so. Next, decide upon dates for regular meetings throughout the PIP period to analyse and discuss performance, rather than waiting until the end to review the entire PIP. Before leaving the meeting, ensure the employee has understood everything you have discussed and has signed the PIP.

The implementation of a PIP often has one of three effects on an employee. The most positive outcome is that the performance improves and the employee

Ask if they feel they need any extra assistance in performing their duties.

Inform the employee of the repercussions of failing to meet the requirements of the PIP and ensure that they are fully aware of the ramifications of doing so.

Decide upon dates for regular meetings throughout the PIP period to analyse and discuss performance.

Ensure the employee has understood everything you have discussed and has signed the PIP.

The implementation of a PIP often has one of three effects on an employee —some improve, some leave the position/company and some do not improve but do not leave.

remains with the company. Alternatively, the employee may feel that they are either unable or unwilling to meet the targets required and will seek to change positions or leave the company. The most unhelpful response, from a manager's point of view at least, is that there is no improvement at all – the employee continues to operate at an unsatisfactory level throughout the PIP process. This inevitably necessitates a difficult conversation with the employee (see Step 8 for more details on handling this) and may even result in the employee's contract being terminated. Of course this is ideally avoided, but managers must use the information provided by the performance measurement tool and the PIP to make a decision on the employee's effectiveness at the company. Situations such as these show why clear, statistically based targets are preferred at the outset.

If the PIP has been implemented properly then it will fall in line with existing HR policy on underperformance, meaning that the employee can have no recourse if they are dismissed on these grounds, providing that the HR policy itself is legally sound (if in any doubt it may be worth investigating the policy's legality before basing your PIP strategy around it). Smaller companies may not have an HR policy in place, in which case the ACAS guidelines on

Employment termination is naturally a last resort, but sometimes poor performers leave the manager with no choice.

Clear, statistically based targets will help you back up your case if it comes to contract termination.

If the PIP has been implemented properly then it will fall in line with existing HR policy on underperformance.

Some companies will not have an HR policy to guide them, in which case the ACAS guidelines can form a legal backbone.

termination of employment can be used as a basis for PIP legalities.

A PIP is naturally a last resort, and on many occasions is not necessary. A quick conversation about performance is all that is normally required with a conscientious and engaged employee to improve performance, but an employee who requires a PIP can illustrate something more serious. More often than not it is down to the individual themselves, but poor performance across a team or department may indicate issues with employee engagement, motivation or other areas of the performance management strategy. An honest and frank conversation with the department members should shed light on this matter and allow bigger steps to be taken, if required.

A quick conversation about performance is all that is normally required with a conscientious and engaged employee to improve performance.

Poor performance across a team or department may indicate issues with employee engagement, motivation or other areas of the performance management strategy.

"Now I ensure staff perform their roles in the way I want them to. If they can't then they have to take on another role, or leave. Seeing this in action sent out a massive signal to all staff. They saw that I was prepared to tackle staff underperformance head on."

Jon Chaloner, headmaster

"Lazy people irritate their employers like vinegar to the teeth or smoke in the eyes."

Proverbs 10:26

"If you do not change direction, you may end up where you are heading."

Lao Tzu

Step 8 – Difficult conversations in the performance management process

As previously mentioned, the success of a performance management strategy depends to a large extent on the qualities and suitability of those employed to implement it – mainly line managers and HR professionals. It naturally follows that not all individuals are suited to all aspects of delivering a performance management strategy, and one of the areas many managers fall down on is that of difficult conversations.

All managers face difficult conversations at some points in their careers, and not all have the instincts, experience or training necessary to deal properly with them. In *Difficult Conversations; 10 Steps to Becoming a Tackler Not a Dodger*, I detailed the steps required to effectively handle a difficult conversation, steps which I will summarise here.

The first stage is to recognise that a discussion has to take place at all. This may seem obvious, but many managers prefer to stick their heads in the sand and hope a problem resolves itself rather than intervene. This only makes the intervention when it comes, as it more than likely will do at some juncture, much more difficult to deal with than if it had been tackled at source. This mentality needs to be reversed swiftly

The success of a performance management strategy depends to a large extent on the qualities and suitability of those employed to implement it.

One of the areas many managers fall down on is that of difficult conversations.

Difficult conversations are a fact of managerial life, but not all managers have the instincts or experience to deal with them.

Hoping a problem resolves itself only makes the inevitable intervention much more difficult to deal with.

before any further steps can be taken. Making a list of the fears associated with tackling such issues may help to rationalise the underlying concerns, from which each concern can be tackled independently. Ironically, those who tend to avoid these confrontations, no matter how small they may be initially, often have a very good radar for detecting the necessity of an upcoming difficult conversation. This, if put to good use, can turn them from a poor manager into a very astute one.

Once the realisation has dawned that a difficult conversation needs to be had, it is time to steal a march by preparing adequately. Naturally one can't prepare for every scenario, but it should be possible to calculate a number of likely outcomes given the nature and character of the employee in question, the severity of the conversation and the topic to be discussed. Using information and data to back up the points being discussed, statistical if possible, is a good way to shield the potential awkwardness of a disciplinary conversation, as it is difficult to argue against facts (again, a well implemented performance measurement tool should be able to assist here).

Importantly, the person having the discussion needs to have a clear idea of what they want out of the discussion before they enter it. Do they need to come out knowing certain information? Are they seeking a

Making a list of the fears associated with tackling such issues may help to rationalise the underlying concerns.

Preparation is the key when it comes to a difficult conversation. Consider the nature and character of the employee in question, the severity of the conversation and the topic to be discussed.

Use information and data extrapolated from the chosen measurement tool to reinforce arguments.

change in the other party's behaviour? Will they be expected to negotiate towards an agreement? Even if the individual is open minded and doesn't know what outcome they want, they need to be prepared so they can work towards an eventual agreement. Keeping in mind what they want to achieve throughout will subconsciously drive body language and tone of voice, whilst conscious thoughts will look after the actual words being spoken.

Keeping the desired outcome in mind will subconsciously drive the direction of the discussion towards the intended goal.

In the build up to the conversation, it is important that the manager is courageous and doesn't back out of the meeting unless it is absolutely vital. Rescheduling at the last minute or avoiding the discussion entirely without a completely valid reason can seem like weakness which can spread through the team and thus amount to a loss of trust and faith in the manager. Some managers opt for email or telephone based measures rather than talking face to face, which not only displays weakness but also demonstrates a lack of respect to the other party. Once a conversation of this nature has been properly tackled once, further difficult conversations will become easier and easier. Getting over this initial hump is the hardest part but brings the biggest reward.

Ensure that the individual who called the meeting does not get cold feet and cancel it. This can seem like a weakness and spreads mistrust.

Ensure the meeting happens face to face and not over the phone or by email.

When actually in the meeting itself, the individual holding it should keep the idiom 'it's not what you say that matters but how you say it' at the forefront of

Remember that 'it's not what you say that matters but how you say it'.

their exchanges. As a starting point, they should put themselves in the position of the person they are due to have the discussion with. How would they like to be addressed about the matter? What specific words or terms would they not want to hear? What would make them either clam up or spill the beans? Remaining calm and professional is vital, as is keeping a little professional distance. Informing someone that their employment is being terminated can bring completely unexpected responses, but, again, the individual should think how they would like to be treated in a similar situation and act accordingly. In some situations it may be necessary to show some compassion, but remember that the employee may not necessarily want compassion from the person who has just delivered the bad news.

A key feature in all employee/manager conversations, but one that is overlooked far too often, is listening. Many line managers fail to listen properly to what team members are telling them, or fail to act on what they are told, which will only have one result in the end – a breakdown in communication and trust from the team to the manager. Employee feedback is key to a successful performance management strategy, and so thoughts, worries or complaints should be listened to with understanding – especially in a difficult conversation where a new way of working may need to

Remaining calm and professional is vital, as is keeping a little professional distance.

In some situations it may be necessary to show some compassion, but remember that the employee may not necessarily want compassion from the person who has just delivered the bad news.

Listening is a critical yet vastly overlooked aspect of communication. Many line managers fail to listen properly to what team members are telling them, or fail to act on what they are told.

Employee feedback is key to a successful performance management strategy, and so thoughts, worries or complaints should be listened to with understanding.

be arranged. The best managers are able to read between the lines and can detect underlying issues which are impacting performance. Not everyone can do this, but being attentive to all aspects of an employee during these discussions, from body language to what is actually being said (or not said), can allow such issues to be detected.

The note that the meeting is left on is also important. If the discussion has some negative aspects to it but the manager wishes to push the employee to improve their performance, then it should end on a positive note with the manager displaying faith that the employee can turn their performance around, that they will always be there for support and that their role in the company is just as important as everyone else's. Ending meetings in this manner is much more effective than ending with details of potential punitive actions if performance doesn't improve.

Being attentive to all aspects of an employee during these discussions, from body language to what is actually being said (or not said), can allow underlying feelings to be detected.

It is important, especially if the subject matter of the meeting has been negative, to leave on a positive note.

Show you have faith in the employee to turn their performance around.

"Courage is what it takes to stand up and speak; courage is also what it takes to sit down and listen."

Winston Churchill

"Tact is the art of making a point without making an enemy."

Sir Isaac Newton

"Professionalism: it's not the job you do, it's how you do the job."

Anonymous

Step 9 – Nudging towards performance management

'Nudge' is a theory put forward by Richard Thaler and Cass Sunstein in their book *Nudge: Improving Decisions about Health, Wealth, and Happiness*. The theory suggests that human beings by and large want to do the 'right thing' in various situations but are too lazy or otherwise not inclined to do it by themselves (quit smoking, recycle, walk to the shops instead of driving etc.). If the 'right thing' is made the most attractive of a number of options then we are more likely to choose that option. This means that those in positions of power can make certain subtle alterations in order to encourage those that they oversee into their chosen direction.

Governments have been quick to utilise this idea – indeed, Barack Obama and David Cameron are known advocates. In Austria, for example, a change in the organ donor scheme from an opt-in scheme to an opt-out one hugely increased the amount of organ donations in one fell swoop; the government made the most desirable option the most attractive. Some opponents claim that this type of intervention is too controlling, and in fact Swedish health authorities have attempted a different approach by calling for the government to contribute towards funerals of those who are registered organ donors. Both these schemes, although approached in different ways, follow the

Nudge theory proposes that it is possible to change the behaviour of a group of people by using human beings' innate desire to do the right thing.

If the 'right thing' is made the most attractive of a number of options then we are more likely to choose that option.

A change in Austrian organ donor policy from an opt-in scheme to an opt-out one hugely increased the amount of organ donations in one fell swoop.

Swedish health authorities have attempted a different approach by calling for the government to contribute towards funerals of those who are registered organ donors.

same premise of using incentives to get people to change their behaviour 'on their own' rather than telling them they have to change something.

Nudge theory has been used in advertising for decades, but only recently have we seen it applied to the private sector. Reports indicate that a large majority of companies tend to use nudge theory for matters such as encouraging recycling by reducing the amount of rubbish bins in offices or cutting the number of sick days by offering staff discounted gym membership, free flu jabs and the like. With the scale of applications nudge theory has to business and the number of practitioners growing, businesses are beginning to see just what nudge theory can do for them – and performance management is no different.

Whilst nudge theory may not be suitable in all areas of performance management strategy planning, it can certainly play a part in many facets that have been discussed in this book. Like many other aspects of performance management, planning and implementing 'nudges' will be a highly individualised process and not everyone involved in the planning will be in a position to put into practice the subtleties and nuances required for it to succeed. Don't forget that this is less a business practice and more a psychological tactic that involves subtly edging people toward certain behaviours, so clearly it must be handled delicately by

So far, nudge theory has mainly been applied on a small scale, such as encouraging recycling and improving employee health and well-being.

Businesses are beginning to see just what nudge theory can do for them – and performance management is no different.

Planning and implementing 'nudges' will be a highly individualised process and not everyone involved in the planning will be suited to implementing it.

the right individuals. If it is done too subtly then there may be no effect, whereas if implementation is too heavy-handed it will defeat the object.

The variety of approaches to practical implementation of nudge theory is only limited by the creativity of the individuals responsible for doing so. As in the organ donor examples earlier, some applications will include a more hands-on approach that actually involves intervening and making an immediate physical change to a system or process, whereas some will be more subtle suggestive efforts that have no obvious consequence but effect the change required. An example of this latter approach, cited by Thaler and Sunstein themselves, is that by putting a frowning face sticker on electricity bills of above average users actually led them to reduce their usage to average or below. This seemingly innocuous addition to the residents' bills had an almost overwhelming effect, as was intended.

Implementation into performance management

So how can these ideas be implemented into performance management? The most obvious way is the way in which the news of a performance management strategy is communicated to staff. As we have already discussed, performance management isn't appreciated by all, and some employees and managers may be hesitant to get on board with the

If nudge theory is applied too subtly then there may be no effect, whereas if implementation is too heavy-handed it will defeat the object.

The variety of approaches to practical implementation of nudge theory is only limited by the creativity of the individuals responsible for doing so.

Some applications will involve a more hands-on approach while others will be more subtle suggestive efforts.

process — something that is vital to the success of performance management. The key is to get employees to actively want to take part in the scheme, something that can be done by carefully tempting them with ideas of individualised rewards, more stake in company success and increased development for top performers — in short, advertising the scheme to them so it is impossible to resist. More people will therefore be accepting of the scheme than if it was simply announced to them.

Nudge theory can be used to slowly introduce the idea of performance management itself and make it seem attractive rather than just announcing it one day.

The promise of greater reward for top performers is a great example of nudge theory's use in performance management. By stating that top performers will receive, say, further career and personal development, mentoring and more individualised rewards, the chances are that you would find improved performance across the board. At the other end of the scale, whilst dismissing someone for poor performance isn't the most pleasant of tasks it will probably have the knock on effect of raising the performance bar across the rest of the team; the dismissal acts as a reminder to all employees of the ramifications of poor performance.

Nudge theory can also be used to increase performance in a number of ways.

Subtly illustrating the benefits of success and the perils of failure will often improve performance across the board whilst not making it obvious that you're trying to do just that.

Nudge theory can also benefit companies in other ways. If for example you want to increase productivity whilst keeping costs down you could publicise a number of appealing non-financial bonuses and

Non-financial bonuses and rewards are a good way to increase performance without extra expense.

rewards. This could also tie in with an employee engagement policy in that employees could vote and choose which rewards they would like each period. Moving to an employee ownership model similar to the retailer John Lewis, could also be something to consider. The thing to remember about nudge theory is that the simplest ideas work the best. Trying to second or third guess your employees will lead to complications and ineffective implementation, whilst the simplest ideas, such as praising good work or subtly recounting another team's impressive results, can have a huge effect on performance. The key thing to remember is that such practices should be delicate and not forced – you are trying to subtly bring out your employees' in-built desire to succeed and perform by tempting them to do better and allowing as much autonomy in the process as possible.

Simplicity is the watchword when it comes to nudge theory; trying to second or third guess your employees will lead to ineffective implementation.

Praising good work or subtly recounting another team's impressive results can have a huge effect on performance.

Remember that you are trying to subtly bring out your employees' in-built desire to succeed by tempting them to do better and allowing as much autonomy in the process as possible.

"Small and apparently insignificant details can have major impacts on people's behaviours. A good rule of thumb is to assume that 'everything matters'."

Richard Thaler & Cass Sunstein, 'Nudge: Improving Decisions About Health, Wealth and Happiness'

"The proper authority saw to it that the proper belief should be induced, and the people believed properly."

Charles Fort

"We perceive and are affected by changes too subtle to be described."

Henry David Thoreau

Step 10 – Next steps

Having evaluated the important elements of a performance management strategy, the next stage is to consider what steps should follow. The first thing you need to ensure is that implementing a performance management strategy is right for your organisation. It can be a great tool for improving huge areas of the business, but it is not a panacea for all business problems . It may be that your business model itself is flawed, in which case a performance management strategy will not get you back in line. It is also true that certain elements of an organisation will not benefit from performance management as much as others. For example, if your organisation requires monotonous manual work by unskilled/semi-skilled individuals, consider whether investment in performance management for this area of the business will be of benefit. Using the outlines provided in this book, and perhaps conducting further research into certain areas will ensure that you can match up the issues which have caused you to investigate performance management with what performance management can actually achieve. If you can't then the time may not be right to yet do so.

Once you are satisfied that a performance management strategy is what's required then it is important to know exactly what outcomes you expect

Performance management can be a great tool for improving huge areas of the business, but it is not a panacea for all business problems.

Ensure that you can match up the issues which have caused you to investigate performance management with what performance management can actually achieve.

It is important to know exactly what outcomes you expect and by when before you begin.

A performance management strategy is not a quick fire solution, so small incremental changes should be sought as indicators of change rather than instant results.

and by when. This will be touched on in your action plan, but prior to this it is important to have an overall idea in your mind of what you would like to change and how long you are willing to give it before these changes are realised. As we have seen, a performance management strategy is not a quick fire solution, so small incremental changes should be sought as indicators of change rather than instant results. This is where the benefit of a quantitative measurement system comes into place; if you have clear, identified methods of collecting good quality data then measuring the stages of change should be relatively easy. If the changes can't be quantified, designing your own measurement metrics will be essential if you are to monitor the changes effectively. Either way, the decision to create a performance management framework represents a turning point for your business, the first step in your new direction.

Implementation

There are a number of ways a business can set about planning and implementing a performance management strategy. The first option is to hire performance management consultants to analyse your business and your requirements and tailor a strategy accordingly. This is probably the most effective method but one that requires a financial investment, so smaller organisations may have to weigh up the cost versus the

If you have clear, identified methods of collecting good quality data then measuring the stages of change should be relatively easy.

The decision to create a performance management framework represents a turning point for your business, the first step in your new direction.

Hiring performance management consultants is the most effective method of implementation.

Using consultants is best suited to medium-sized and large companies.

potential reward before embarking on such a path. Users of this approach can expect practitioners to work with the company on and off-site for some months as the process moves from planning through implementation and troubleshooting stages until line managers and HR can take over the reins. This is the most desirable option for medium-sized to large companies. Some consultancy organisations might be willing to link the increase in performance to their fee structure.

An alternative already discussed in Step 2 is to use computer software to serve the purpose. Whilst experts will be required to set up the software and train users, once this is done the users can control everything from there, viewing and extracting data where required, easily evaluating progress and identifying areas of underperformance, all at the click of a button. Some software systems offer a more complete service than others however; 'Work Manager' for example helps companies track productivity down to the minute while others focus more on progress towards goals and targets. Those looking at the software only route therefore will have to ensure that they will get everything they need from their chosen package. Advantages to this method include lower financial outlay and a higher sense of autonomy from the outset, but a software only

Specialist computer software can also serve the purpose.

Users can view and extract performance data where required, easily evaluating progress and identifying areas of underperformance.

A software only approach doesn't usually offer as much all-round integration as the consultant approach, but it is usually more cost-effective.

approach doesn't usually offer as much all-round integration as the consultant approach. Employees can also feel that they are being too heavily monitored and some may resent having to log their activities on a daily or even hourly basis. This approach is best suited to companies who want to hire experts but are on tighter budgetary restrictions.

The software approach is best suited to companies who want to hire experts but are on tighter budgetary restrictions.

The third option is the DIY approach – to train existing members of staff (or to hire someone exclusively for the purpose) in the art of performance management and have them design and implement the strategy in-house. This approach is often better suited to smaller organisations where budgets can allow for training but not hiring external assistance. The biggest risk with this method is the pressure placed on those responsible for the implementation and training. A business utilising this method needs to have absolute confidence in that individual/team, but can look forward to a cut-price performance management strategy.

Companies on even smaller budgets can train existing staff in performance management.

The DIY approach can put pressure on those chosen to implement it, but if done well it can prove to be very effective at a fraction of the cost of hiring consultants.

Action plan

Once you have decided which option you would like to pursue you can go about creating an action plan. This document should use the information you have gathered from your chosen provider to set out time frames and milestones related to the implementation of the framework. All action plans are different, but following there is a guide of the types of areas that will

The next step is to draw up an action plan. This document sets out time frames and milestones related to the implementation of the framework.

need to be addressed as part of the plan. These areas are:

Aim: The overall target

Action: The individual components that will allow the aim to be met

Sub-action: The tasks required to complete each action

Timescale: The approximate date by when the action should be completed

Responsibility: Which group/individual is responsible for carrying out the action

Some organisations also include a rating system to score the success of each step, whilst others plan short-term, midterm and long-term goals separately. Whichever method you adopt, remember that a performance management strategy is not a quick fix for a particular workplace problem, rather it represents a complete change in attitude and approach towards the organisation and the tasks performed. This attitude should emanate from the top and should be cascaded down the organisation to entry-level employees and potential job applicants. The benefits of implementing a performance management framework are manifold, ranging from improved employee performance and corporate alignment to an increase in job satisfaction across the company and, most importantly, an increase in the bottom line. A properly implemented

Remember that a performance management strategy is not a quick fix for a particular workplace problem but a complete change in attitude.

This attitude should be cascaded down through every level of the organisation.

A properly implemented performance management strategy not only acts in the short-term to identify and help rectify problems but it also helps to maintain performance and prevent such issues occurring in the future.

performance management strategy is invaluable as it not only acts in the short-term to identify and help rectify areas of underperformance but it also helps to maintain performance and prevent such issues occurring in the future. The road to get there isn't always smooth, but persistence pays off immeasurably.

A key point to remember regarding the planning and implementation of a performance management strategy is that it is a long-term process and as such cannot be rushed. Results cannot be expected immediately and users should not lose heart if the desired milestones are missed; teething problems are natural, but as long as the right people are involved in the process then any obstacles can be overcome. As we have seen it is a highly integrated system with many facets feeding off and interlinking with each other, and it is for this reason that enlisting the help of professionals in the field is highly recommended; a poorly implemented performance management strategy can do more to damage staff morale and performance than if nothing had been attempted in the first place.

Remember that instant results are rare and cannot be expected – but don't lose heart!

Given the complexity of implementing a performance management strategy it is advisable that, even if you can't hire them, you at least speak to professionals.

"Any change, even a change for the better, is always accompanied by drawbacks and discomforts."

Arnold Bennett

"We delight in the beauty of the butterfly, but rarely admit the changes it has gone through to achieve that beauty"

Maya Angelov

"A year from now you will wish you had started today."

Karen Lamb

Conclusion

Hopefully this handbook has given you an insight into the essentials of performance management and how to apply them to your organisation. Ideally it will have also shown you the myriad of advantages to implementing a performance management strategy regardless of an organisation's size.

The following is a breakdown of each step which may be useful for reference:

1. The essentials

Performance management is commonly split into four categories:

Organisational performance management

Corporate strategies and goals are discussed and departmental goals set

Department performance management

Departmental goals are discussed with team leaders and team goals are set

Team performance management

Team goals are passed down to employees

Individual performance management

Employees are performance managed to ensure that they are meeting their individual goals

Organisational frameworks will differ from company to company, but each stratum must have its own goals and performance management strategies in place to ensure global success. The Plan – Action – Review – Revise cycle should be adhered to as much as possible. Performance management applies to systems and processes too, not just the human workforce.

2. Goal setting and measuring

Follow the SMART acronym when setting goals:

- Specific
- Measurable
- Achievable
- Realistic
- Time based

As well as standard goals, stretch objectives can motivate employees to push themselves above and beyond for extra reward and satisfaction.

The Balanced Scorecard is a recognised system for measuring many aspects of organisational performance, but specialist software is becoming increasingly better suited to the needs of companies looking at implementing a performance management strategy. Companies can define their own measurement metrics, but easily extractable quantitative data is ideal as it makes analysing performance very easy.

Regular review meetings are vital to ensure performance management success. They allow you to recognise and deal with performance issues before they take hold, ensure that employees are happy in their work and have everything they need to do their jobs to the best of their ability and allow target tweaking if necessary.

3. Reward strategies

Monetary rewards alone are now less desired than ever, and what the majority of employees now want is respect, trust and a sense of fulfilment at work. Reward strategies should be tailored to individuals for ultimate benefit and should include a combination of monetary and more personal rewards. Rewards should also be discussed and agreed with employees, who will then have much more of a stake in their own success which will almost always result in a rise in performance levels.

There are generally two styles of employee motivation when it comes to reward:

Extrinsic

Extrinsic rewards are those that involve some external motivation on behalf of the employee, for example money, status and power. Extrinsic rewards often take the form of a salary increase or bonus, time off, improved work environment or conditions (new car, bigger office, etc.), promotion or more job security.

Intrinsic

Intrinsic rewards are based around personal fulfilment, job satisfaction and the knowledge of contribution to overall success of the individual. Examples of intrinsic motivations can include further recognition/awards, further training/personal development, higher profile projects and equipment to do their jobs better.

Ensure team managers enter into dialogue with employees in order to ascertain what motivates them, thus allowing them to tailor rewards accordingly and therefore raise the performance bar. Ensure that underperformers don't receive similar rewards to those performing well; they need to be motivated, but fairness is the watchword when it comes to reward strategies.

4. The appraisal

The annual/biannual appraisal has two aspects – the past and the future. In the first place it should tie up all the regular reviews over the desired period and assess overall performance in relation to the goals set during the last appraisal, through which the agreed rewards should be apportioned. The next period's goals and rewards should also be agreed, whilst using the opportunity to strengthen employee engagement if possible.

The appraisal structure should be as follows:

- Introduction stating appraisal purpose
- Review of past objectives and reward apportioning
- Implementation of Personal Improvement Plan if necessary
- Discussion of employee concerns or extra requirements
- Reminder of employee importance in overall operation – strengthening of employee engagement
- Discussion and agreement of future objectives and rewards

The individual being appraised will expect the following outcomes from their appraisal:

- Receive constructive feedback on all aspects of their performance
- Be made aware what their career prospects are for the period and in the future
- Be able to air grievances about management or the organisation without it affecting their prospects
- Be able to discuss salary frankly
- Understand what their objectives are for the period ahead
- Above all, to feel notice has been taken of what they have said

Studies have shown that many employees rate trust in their line manager as the most important motivational factor, so ensure that you tackle appraisals fairly and honestly but that the employee leaves with their importance to the company and their own self-worth heightened.

5. Performance management and employee engagement

Employee engagement is an extension of the phrase 'job satisfaction'. This is becoming increasingly important to employees and so should be equally important to line managers and heads of department. Employee engagement increases employee happiness and fulfilment, which in turn increases motivation, performance, discretionary effort and more.

The following four factors drive employee engagement:

Trust

Employees rate trust in their line manager very highly and it can have a huge impact on performance. In basic terms, an employee who doesn't trust their line manager won't work as hard for them. Recent spates of redundancies have strained this trust to breaking point, but a manager who deals with such issues fairly and professionally will not lose the trust of his or her staff.

Learning and development

Employees need to feel that the company is not just supporting the work they are doing at that moment but is actively supporting their development, both personal and career wise. Well advertised and successful internal promotion fosters in-house motivation and a higher calibre of external candidate, whilst a company that helps its employees expand their lives outside of work strengthens that bond and therefore raises motivation.

Meaningful and engaging work

Employees should have the feeling that the work they are doing matters, especially if it is typically repetitive or mundane work. Some work is naturally engaging and meaningful, but that which isn't must have meaning attached to it somewhere as employees need to feel that what they do matters. If the work itself cannot be made meaningful, then the result of that work should have meaning in the overall company operation and the employee should be made aware of this.

Fair and fulfilling reward

Employees need to be adequately rewarded for their work for motivation and performance to remain high. The more tailored these rewards are to the individual the better the results will be. Sometimes a simple unexpected 'well done' can have a more positive impact on performance than an entire package of tailored rewards.

Remember to involve trade unions from the outset and listen to their views on your intentions. They will want to ensure that you are not simply trying to increase discretionary effort and that their members won't be adversely affected by any changes.

6. Performance management and talent management

Retaining and developing top talent is one of the fundamental keys to success in business. Employee engagement strategies play a huge part in this, but top performers may have to be treated differently. A clear, quantitative performance measurement system can easily help you identify top performers in one sense, but managers who have the ability to see skills outside the usual sphere may help deploy employees elsewhere for maximum effect.

Talent management strategies should be aligned with corporate strategies to ensure the organisation as a whole doesn't suffer because of trying to keep one star performer happy. Talent management can be split into four categories:

Focus: Decide what you are looking for. What kind of people will help drive your company in the direction you want?

Identify: Identify top performers using your performance measurement tools and speak to managers to identify potential stars in other parts of the company.

Plan: Plant the seed of potential development and tap into their personal desires and ambitions. Allow them to realise they can achieve their potential within your company but don't force the idea on them too soon.

Manage and develop: Invest in their development and ensure that their performance is monitored each step of the way, grooming them for certain positions if they show interest and aptitude.

Top performers will already be in your employee engagement plans, but paying extra attention to their satisfaction and ambitions will only help. Don't smother them, but subtly ensure that they are happy on the path they are going and also that they are performing to the level anticipated. Top performers often like to be challenged, so show faith in them and you will be rewarded much more often than not.

7. Performance improvement plans

A performance improvement plan (PIP) is an agreement drawn up by an underperforming individual and their manager that clearly sets out areas of required improvement, capability and timelines associated with them. The structure is generally as follows:

Determination of underperformance: Underperformance is detected using the chosen performance measurement tool.

PIP intention notice issued: The employee is notified of his or her underperformance and is informed that a PIP will be implemented.

PIP implemented: A PIP is drawn up and the employee is made aware of required improvements and consequences of continued underperformance.

Determination of improvement: Employee performance is monitored for change in line with agreed targets and timelines and relevant action taken if improvement is not satisfactory.

The more specific you can be with the required areas and levels of improvement then the easier it will be for the employee to aim for them and the manager to measure them. Targets should be discussed and agreed with the employee, but consequences of failure should be in line with standard HR policy and not adjusted. Ensure that your HR policy is legally sound before embarking on a PIP. If in any doubt, or if you don't have a HR policy, consult the ACAS guidelines. Remember the basic principle of treating everyone with dignity and respect here.

8. Difficult conversations in the performance management process

Difficult conversations are an inevitable part of the performance management process, and some managers are better able to deal with them than others. The following tips will help those who find difficult conversations hard to tackle:

- **Recognise** that a discussion needs to happen by spotting underperformance through measurement tools.
- **Prepare** for the conversation using data and any related feedback about the subject.
- **Plan** how you want the meeting to end and what result you want and steer the conversation in that direction.
- **Be courageous**, see the meeting through as planned.
- **Be professional**, strong and fair in the meeting.
- **Listen** to what the employee is saying, don't just reel off your list of points.
- **Leave the meeting on a positive light**, focusing on the potential for improvement and ideally with the employee motivated to turn things round.

9. Nudging towards performance management

Nudge theory is the idea that permanent shifts in behaviour can be brought around by seemingly insignificant changes that are in fact carefully calculated to use human beings' natural desire to do the 'right thing'. It suggests that when faced with decisions, a 'right' (or desired) option will usually be chosen but only if it is made more appealing than the alternatives. Most of us, it is claimed, do want to do the right thing but are often too lazy to do it. The key then is to carefully make the desired choice the easiest to pick, that way behaviour can be influenced to fit, say, a new corporate vision or way of working.

Nudge theory can be utilised in a performance management setting in a number of ways, from communicating the news of the impending implementation to staff motivation and goal setting. Ideally, specialist practitioners should be hired to implement nudge theory, as some mistaken attempts from amateurs can actually make things worse. It is important to offer as much autonomy as possible whilst guiding employees in a certain direction as they will be less likely to adopt a new routine or change their thinking if they feel they are being forced into it.

Whilst it can be a slightly overawing prospect to plan and implement a performance management strategy from scratch, tackling it in the same manner as I have tackled it in this book will allow you to break down the process into manageable sections and ensure that each measure is implemented properly, targets are achieved and nothing is overlooked. It is without doubt a large undertaking, but it should be seen as an investment rather than simply an exercise. With the right systems and the right people in place, a performance management strategy will allow your business to focus on its strengths, iron out its weaknesses and allow you to forge something that will hold you in good stead through both smooth and choppy financial waters – a dedicated, motivated workforce working towards clear, established goals. I wish you good luck.

Case studies

The following case studies outline how performance management can influence businesses in all sectors when correctly implemented.

Brewsters Retail

Matthew Simons took over as the CEO of Brewsters, a large multi-site electrical retail chain two years ago. Sales in the year prior to his arrival were £425m, down 10% on the previous year. The company employs just over 5000 staff. There were many significant factors for Brewsters to contend with. These included:

- Increasing costs of business regulation
- Constant competitor activity
- A consumer move towards online shopping
- A mix of good and bad store locations
- Increasing levels of global sourcing challenges
- Higher customer service demands from customers

The business had been trading for 60 years and had built a good brand and a solid reputation but upon his arrival Matthew realised that fortunes had to be reversed. He put six initiatives in place to grow the business, one of which was a performance management system, something that had been in place previously but that had steadily fallen into decline. Matthew and the HR Director met and decided to reinvigorate the scheme and relaunch it. The scheme comprised:

- Six monthly appraisal sessions
- Line manager training on one-to-one and appraisal discussions
- The introduction of weekly one-to-ones
- Objective clarification meetings for all senior managers

Within six months of implementation, like for like sales were up 14% up on the previous year, and within two years the business had achieved compound growth of 19% with employee turnover falling and mystery shopper results improving. Each change had played its part; the six monthly appraisals and weekly one-to-ones allowed tighter monitoring of staff performance, the training allowed managers to make staff meetings and appraisals more effective and productive and the objective clarification sessions resolved a number of overlapping managerial responsibilities. Matthew puts his success down to organisation wide focus:

"The whole organisation was focused on improving performance and actively had regular discussions about what we could do rather than pretending it wasn't happening. If everyone is on board the whole process has much more chance of success."

Cardwell Hospital

Cardwell Hospital employs some 4000 staff. The Chief Executive had been in the post for just over three years and upon taking over was faced with frequent complaints from both staff and patients about the amount of agency nurses being used and wards and other services being short-staffed. To make matters worse, the local paper had also been running stories about infection levels on wards of the hospital.

The records showed that the hospital had a staff sickness absence level of 6% which was double the target, around 45% of which was attributable to stress related problems, resulting in huge extra cost to the hospital. The effects of these absences were also seen in the hospital targets; there was a regular breach in the number of A&E patients waiting more than the target four hours to be seen, whilst the 18 week hospital operation admission target was also frequently missed.

To get to the bottom of the problem, the Chief Executive commissioned a staff survey, to which 2300 employees responded. 34% indicated broad job dissatisfaction, with the most stressful demands relating to work overload, organisational demands, role ambiguity and problems in the work environment. 25% of respondents were considering leaving the job. Staff in high strain positions (high demands and low control) had the highest levels of work induced stress. The results also showed that staff received support from the following sources:

- Family and friends (81%)
- Colleagues (79%)
- Other professionals (57%)
- Managers (51%)
- Patients/clients (38%)
- Community resources (29%)

Recognising that stress, sickness and staff dissatisfaction levels were posing a real threat to the organisation's performance, the Chief Executive embarked on a programme to turn the situation around. She began a process of clarifying roles and responsibilities, underpinned by clarifying the organisation's objectives. As part of the role clarification process, all those with people management responsibility were asked to attend a two day 'managing people' workshop. Some clinical staff expressed reluctance in engaging in the process but the Chief Executive made it mandatory. The process was completed within six months and raised a number of important issues relating to operations management which explained why national targets were regularly being breached. Changes in procedure were discussed and implemented.

Heads of service were then invited to provide a review of performance for each of their departments in monthly sessions. As a result of the shift in focus towards performance, 40% of the senior team resigned, were demoted or moved into different jobs, thus streamlining the departments and allowing them to work more efficiently. Network groups were also set up to increase the level of peer group support available.

Within a year, the hospital had improved dramatically. National targets began to be met, and a similar survey 18 months later showed marked improvements in staff and patient satisfaction levels. The Chief Executive partially attributes this success to strong leadership:

"I met with resistance from a number of senior figures at various stages of the process, but I knew that what I was doing was right and would work so I didn't alter anything. We lost some good people, but many of them saw fairly early that their positions were adversely affecting hospital performance. Some were integrated somewhere else, some resigned or retired and some had to be made redundant. It was tough but necessary, and the results speak for themselves. Ultimately, the patients come first."

Network High Senior School

Network High Senior School is an inner city school with 1300 pupils from a broad range of socio-economic and racial backgrounds. Hilary had been Head Teacher for three years and in that time the school had come a long way; in the previous year 41% of pupils had achieved A*-C GCSE grades. However, one area that continued to underperform was mathematics (the last set of results had shown only 17% of pupils achieved A*-C GCSE grades in this subject).

The Department Head, Barry Smith, had been at the school for nearly 15 years, having started as a Maths Teacher and been promoted to Head of Department five years ago. Hilary knew that she needed to talk to Barry about the school's maths performance but had kept putting off the discussion because of other issues surrounding him and his work; he was regularly late, poorly dressed and neglectful in many of his line management responsibilities such as having regular reviews with staff. Hilary knew that if she was going to tackle the departmental underperformance she would have to tackle these issues as well, and the prevailing wisdom of the time from parents and other teachers was "that's just how Barry is". The subject, unsurprisingly, had been too lengthy for discussion at the previous three Governors' meetings.

A combination of two things acted as the catalyst for Hilary to deal with the situation; a damning Ofsted report on the department and her attendance of a training course on tackling difficult conversations. Presently she met with the union representative and discussed her concerns. To her surprise the union representative was empathetic and supportive.

When the time came to have the conversation with Barry, Hilary listed all her areas of concern and stated that the time had come to do something about them. She then outlined the corrective action she would be taking, the results she expected to see and the timescales she wanted them completed in. Some were immediate changes involving Barry and his approach whilst others were longer term targets in the academic performance of maths students. Barry reacted badly to these suggestions, quickly becoming angry and aggressive and shouting at Hilary, accusing her of victimisation. After 30 minutes he got up and walked out of the meeting.

The following day Barry failed to turn up for work and in fact didn't return until four weeks later when he called Hilary and asked if he could come in and see her that afternoon. In the meeting Barry informed Hilary that he had decided to move on from the school; an opportunity had come up for a teaching job elsewhere, minus the department head responsibilities, and he was going to take it. When asked about the conversation that had sparked his absence his response was that he had been surprised that Hilary had finally decided to tackle him about it.

Within months of Barry leaving a new Head of Maths was in place, and within a year the number of pupils achieving A*-C GCSE grades for maths had jumped to 43%. Hilary was delighted, as were the governors, other teachers and parents. The reputation of both the school and Hilary herself were greatly enhanced, and Hilary's only regret is that she didn't tackle it sooner:

"If I had dealt with the obvious problems the moment I had spotted them then much of the aggravation could have been avoided. In the end various other issues compounded the poor performance of the department, and the longer I left it the more difficult it became to tackle the individual as the problems seemed too huge and long-standing to challenge. The experience taught me a valuable lesson, and now I nip things in the bud as soon as I can rather than leaving them to grow out of proportion. I've discovered the hard way there are no advantages to putting things off."

Note sheet: Things I will do differently as a result of reading this book

Note sheet: Things I will do differently as a result of reading this book

About the author

Clive Lewis OBE DL

Clive Lewis is a leading Human Resources professional, specialising in employee relations. He is the founding director of Globis Mediation Group and Healthcare HR Solutions. He is the author of several books, including the widely acclaimed "Difficult Conversations – 10 Steps to Becoming a Tackler not a Dodger" and The Definitive Guide to Workplace Mediation. He works across the public, private and voluntary sectors. His work has taken him across four continents and he frequently works at Government level. He was recently appointed as a UK mediation expert to Jordan.

Clive is a non-executive Director in the NHS, a Trustee of the National Youth Jazz Orchestra and the E-Act Group of Academies, Chair of the Open College Network South West and Honorary Secretary of the Civil Mediation Council.

He is also heavily involved in charity work and devotes much of his time to helping young people from poor socio-economic backgrounds. His commitment to charity work led to him being appointed as Chair of a Government-appointed independent panel exploring the rising costs of youth underachievement. He was awarded an OBE for public service in the Queen's Birthday Honours list of 2011. He was also commissioned as a Deputy Lieutenant in 2012.

Appendix I – 1st Generation Balanced Scorecard

Workshop - How to Manage Performance

A high impact workshop covering the key content areas of this handbook is available. The content is highly interactive and the facilitators help delegates understand how to implement the key principles associated with Performance Management.

Context

- Is performance management on your list of responsibilities?
- Are you struggling to manage poor performers?
- Are you nervous about managing different people with different needs?
- Could your skills and confidence benefit from a day of practical training?

Managing performance is one of the biggest concerns to managers across all sectors and industries. The responsibility of getting the best results from individuals can cause concern for managers and is an increasingly critical part of the role in a time where you may well be being demanded to deliver more with less resource.

Aims

This one day course will equip delegates with the skills and confidence to effectively understand the aims of performance management. Participants will gain an understanding of acceptable standards of performance and be able to utilise performance management tools to enhance the performance of their teams, and the individuals within them.

Workshop content

- Understanding performance management
- Maintaining authority and respect
- Managing poor performance
- Managing high performance
- Defining key performance measures and putting them in place
- Structuring expectations
- Recognising and closing performance gaps
- How to set SMART objectives
- Motivating your team

Who should attend?

This course will be of benefit to anyone working in a team leader, supervisor or manager capacity with the responsibility for enhancing the performance, engagement and conduct of individuals or teams. The content of this course is suitable for participants from all sectors and industries.

To book a training course or to find out more about other training programmes, call 0330 100 0809 or visit www.globis.co.uk

Order form

Performance Management
Ten Steps to Getting the Most from Your Workforce

Book Quantity	Price
1-14 copies	£9.99 each
15-29 copies	£7.99 each
30-99 copies	£5.99 each
100-999 copies	£5.75 each
1,000-4,999 copies	£5.50 each
5,000-9,999 copies	£5.25 each
10,000 or more copies	£5.00 each

Name: .... Job Title: ....

Organisation: ....

Address: ....

Postcode: .... Tel No: ....

Email: ....

(Plus Postage and packing)
□ Cheque enclosed (Please make payable to Globis Ltd)
□ Please invoice
□ Please debit my credit card

Name on card: .... Card Number: ....

Start Date: .... Expiry Date: .... Security No: ....

Signed: ....

Post completed form to: Globis Ltd, Unit 1, Wheatstone Court, Quedgeley, Gloucester GL2 2AQ

Tel: 0330 100 0809
Fax: 01452 726001
Email: info@globis.co.uk

References

1. Abernethy, M.A., Horne, M.H., Lillis, A.M., Malina, M.A. and Selto, F.H., (2005) *A multi-method approach to building causal performance maps from expert knowledge.* Retrieved February 1st 2012 from iteseerx.ist.psu.edu/viewdoc/summary?doi=10.1.1.94.1685.

2. CIPD (2009) *Performance Management in Action: Current Trends and Practice.* Retrieved February 1st 2012 from http://www.cipd.co.uk/ NR/rdonlyres/AC5B3F1D-CA83-4CB2-AD97-9B2333411133/0/ Performance_management_in_action.pdf.

3. Thomas, K. (2009) *The Four Intrinsic Rewards That Drive Employee Engagement.* Ivey Business Journal, November/December 2009.

4. Seijts, Gerard H., Crim, D. (2006) *The Ten C's of Employee Engagement.* Ivey Business Journal, March/April 2006.

5. CIPD (June 2011) *Talent management: an overview.* Retrieved 16th Jan 2012 from http://www.cipd.co.uk/hr-resources/factsheets/talent-management-overview.aspx.

6. Gostick, A., Elton, C. (2009) The Carrot Principle: How the Best Managers Use Recognition to Engage Their People, Retain Talent, and Accelerate Performance. Pocket Books, London.

7. CIPD (2009) Performance Management in Action: Current Trends and Practice. Retrieved January 21st 2012 from http://www.cipd.co.uk/ NR/rdonlyres/AC5B3F1D-CA83-4CB2-AD97-9B2333411133/0/ Performance_management_in_action.pdf.